Afghanistan

Mazar-i-Sharif, near Balkh, in northern Afghanistan, is the setting for this peaceful sunset scene: children playing in the foreground, while behind them, to the right, a man prepares to offer prayers of thanks for the day.

THIS BEAUTIFUL WORLD   VOL. 7

Afghanistan

by MASATOSHI KONISHI

 KODANSHA INTERNATIONAL LTD.
TOKYO, NEW YORK & SAN FRANCISCO

Distributors:

UNITED STATES: *Harper & Row, Publishers, Inc., 10 East 53rd Street, New York, New York 10022.* SOUTH AMERICA: *Harper & Row, International Department.* CANADA: *Fitzhenry & Whiteside Limited, 150 Lesmill Road, Don Mills, Ontario.* MEXICO AND CENTRAL AMERICA: *HARLA S. A. de C. V., Apartado 30-546, Mexico 4, D. F.* BRITISH COMMONWEALTH (*excluding Canada and the Far East*): *TABS, 7 Maiden Lane, London WC2.* EUROPE: *Boxerbooks Inc., Limmatstrasse 111, 8031 Zurich.* AUSTRALIA AND NEW ZEALAND: *Book Wise (Australia) Pty. Ltd., 104–8 Sussex Street, Sydney.* THAILAND: *Central Department Store Ltd., 306 Silom Road, Bangkok.* HONG KONG AND SINGAPORE: *Books for Asia Ltd., 30 Tat Chee Avenue, Kowloon; 65 Crescent Road, Singapore 15.* THE FAR EAST: *Japan Publications Trading Company, P.O. Box 5030, Tokyo International, Tokyo.*

Published by Kodansha International Ltd., 2–12–21 Otowa, Bunkyo-ku, Tokyo 112 and Kodansha International/USA, Ltd., 10 East 53rd Street, New York, New York 10022 and 44 Montgomery Street, San Francisco, California 94104. Copyright © 1963 by Kodansha International Ltd. All rights reserved. Printed in Japan.

LCC 69–16367
ISBN 0–87011–071–3
JBC 0325–780828–2361

First edition, 1963
Second printing, 1975

Contents

Afghanistan

Crossroads of the Ages

It was not, of course, until after we had left Kabul's standardized airport and started our drive toward the city that we felt we were truly in Afghanistan—the other eight members of our group for the first time, I for the second. To be accurate, I was not really a member of the group but had been invited to accompany them as adviser, since I knew the country and had some knowledge of its two commonest languages: Pashto and Persian.

Tokyo University, (where I am in the Department of Cultural Anthropology), had sent the group to make a survey of the Southwest Hindu Kush. Most of the members were students of either engineering or agriculture in the University—six men and two women whose average age was twenty-two. Our aim, aside from the primary one of study and investigation, was to live as much as possible with the people and to get to know them as intimately as possible in the short time at our disposal.

Our group began its study of the two languages almost before our ship was out of sight of Yokohama, and we continued assiduously throughout the long sea voyage to Colombo—for without the ability to communicate, the group was hardly likely to gain much insight into the mind and character of the people. I myself had spent over six months in Pashto villages two years before.

After debarking at Colombo, we took a train to New Delhi and then a plane to Kabul. We were to spend our first month traveling and in the capital and our second in a village. What village it was to be we had not yet decided—and in any case we knew we would need the permission of the government in Kabul and its help not only in the choice of a village but also in securing the cooperation of the villagers.

The road into the city from the airport passes Bemaru Heights, the scene of some of the most exciting events in Afghanistan's long and dramatic history—chiefly, of course, the momentous arrival in October, 1504, of Zehir-uddin Muhammad, who was later to take the name of Babur, the Tiger. The area now called Afghanistan has been fought and disputed over by most of the world's chief conquerors for well over two thousand years, from the Persians in the sixth century B.C. to the British and the Persians in the nineteenth century A.D. (At present, both Russia and America are attempting to woo Afghanistan with economic aid.) Among the earlier invaders were Genghis Khan and Tamerlane—and Babur, who claimed to be a descendant of both.

But the conquistador blood in his veins was not quite hot enough when, at the age of twelve, he inherited his father's kingdom in a small valley east of Samarkand. There was an uprising, he was forced to flee with a few followers, and for a time wandered homeless and throneless over the Hindu Kush. Nine years later, he climbed the heights of Bemaru and looked down upon the city of Kabul, nearly seven thousand feet in altitude and surrounded by peaks twice its height. The boy liked what he saw. The blood had come to a boil: Babur was twenty-one.

He lit flares on the summit to announce his warlike arrival, then with his troops descended on the city. He won it, ruled it—though not always comfortably, and, enchanted by the beauty of the valley, built gardens and palaces. Never in his life, not even after he had gone on to those far more extensive conquests of his in India, did he forget Kabul. In a letter to his son, Kamran, then governor of the city, he wrote: "I can never erase from my heart the delights of Kabul. Nor can I express the depth of my longing to return."

He did eventually return. The founder of the Mughal Empire lies buried in one of his favorite gardens in Kabul. The simplicity of the tomb of this remarkable man is in itself unforgettably impressive.

After leaving Bemaru and continuing toward the center of town, one passes the Royal Palace, called the Arg (the Turkish word for "citadel"), built by the Amir Abdur Rahman Khan in 1883, which ever since has served as a residence for the kings of Afghanistan, including the reigning monarch, His Majesty Muhammad Zahir Shah. The airport road, which is lined by plane trees, ends at Pakhtunistan Square, with a huge fountain lit by colored lights at night, and an outdoor cafe. Here, too, stands the Ministry of Information, which was to prove so helpful to us. Many varieties of flowers—dahlias, zinnias, marigolds—were in bloom beneath the plane trees.

The square and surrounding streets were crowded with strollers —the population of the city is almost half a million—and it was not the clothes they wore that told us they were Afghans. With their well-tailored suits and Italian-style shoes, the men might have been government employes in almost any west European city—save for their *karakul* (lambskin) caps and their tall, slender bodies and long faces. The women, too, wore well-cut suits and high-heeled shoes and—to the surprise of many of our group—no *chadris*, as the voluminous, shroud-like veil that muslim women wear is called in this part of the world. Actually the *chadri* is a kind of combination veil, shawl, and head-covering, but the well-dressed ladies of Kabul wore in its place only a sort of neckerchief, which might be a vestige of the traditional fashion.

Shops are well-stocked with imported goods from almost every country of the world, although perhaps the preponderance comes from the Soviet Union and the East European countries. And as in every other city of the world, strollers do their windowshopping as they walk.

Then suddenly a herd of sheep lopes across the street, and one realizes anew that one is in a remote corner of the world—remote now, that is to say, but once very near the center.

As Dr. Arnold J. Toynbee puts it, present-day Afghanistan was once one of the chief "round-abouts" for the spread of civilization from its birthplace in Iraq some five thousand years ago. Opposed to the "round-abouts," in Professor Toynbee's parlance, are the "culs-de-sac," like my own country, Japan. "A long procession of nomadic or ex-nomadic migrant peoples have passed through Afghanistan from Central Asia en route for the Indo-Pakistani subcontinent. The Aryans, who passed through at some date during the second half of the second millennium B.C., brought the Sanskrit language to India. ... A swarm of Iranian-speaking nomadic invaders who occupied the Helmand River basin and the Punjab in the seventh century B.C. deserves mention because one of the participating tribes bore the name Pactyike according to the Ancient Greek historian Herodotus. Is the name that has come down to us in this Ancient Greek version identical with the present-

1. *Pathan driver* waiting for his radiator to cool; men who know how to drive make good money in Afghanistan now.

3—4. *Two mosques,* to suggest the variety of
muslim architecture (since the religion of Islam was
introduced to Afghanistan by the Arabs over a
millennium ago); the crumbling ruin at Chesht
(above) is a deserted reminder of the past, while
the blue mosque at Mazar-i-Sharif (right), today
still magnificently encloses the tomb of Caliph 'Ali.

2. *Valley of Bamiyan,*
photographed from
the grounds of the
hill-top hotel, show-
ing the cliffs where the
two giant Buddhas are
carved and the count-
less caves that served
both as sanctuaries and
dwelling-places for the
monks and priests.

day name Pakhtuns (alias Pathans)? If it is, we have here a clue to the date at which the ancestors of the present-day Pathans first established themselves in the Helmand basin."*

Whatever that date may have been, there is no question that the Pathans are the dominant people in Afghanistan. They form the largest racial group among the country's population of twelve million, and it is they who are generally thought of as the "real Afghans," with their tall frames, long heads, high noses, and their expressions of serene contempt for people less fortunate than they in the matter of birth. The fierce pride of the Pathans and their strong love for their nation—not unlike that of the Vietnamese with their long history of exploitation—inspired the ferocious action that drove back the British colonialists in the nineteenth-century Afghanistan wars, though the independent-minded Afghans were, and are, more fortunate than other exploited Asian nations in possessing a comparatively remote location.

They themselves believe that they are the true Aryans, but most probably the Pathans were of Turko-Iranian origin, with some Indian admixture. Most of them live south of the Hindu Kush; several tribes are largely nomadic, some are farmers, others are sophisticated government officials. In fact, the charge has been made that Kabul, which runs the country, is in turn run by Pathans. The reigning king is from a tribe called the Muhammadzai.

Looking at the faces of a crowd of people in Kabul one day, I was suddenly convinced I saw a fellow Japanese—and then I realized that the man I was looking at was most likely a Hazara from central Afghanistan. The Hazaras are believed to be descendants of Mongols who moved into the region between the thirteenth

*Arnold J. Toynbee, *Between Oxus and Jumna*, (London, 1961).

15

and fifteenth centuries; they inhabit chiefly the high central massif of the country, a region where stony valleys and treeless plateaus make farming arduous. Nonetheless, farming is their chief occupation; when they move to a city, they are likely to become soldiers. Their social status is seldom high. They tend to be simple, rather taciturn people; their language is a dialect of Persian, with considerable Turkish mixed into it.

But there are many other ethnic groups in Afghanistan besides the Pathans and the Hazaras. Despite the smallness of its population, Afghanistan may be likened to the United States in being a melting-pot of different ethnic groups—though the origins of those groups are not always very clear.

Turkish and Turko-Mongolian elements, for instance, have long been present in Afghanistan. Both Turkomans and Uzbeks are Muslims of the Sunnite sect, and both are famous rug-makers, but the Turkomans, who live in dome-shaped tents, are largely sheep breeders, while the Uzbeks are sedentary villagers whose main occupations are farming and trading. They comprise the majority of the population in and around Kunduz. Their carpets, which are famous the world over, are expensive even in Afghanistan, because they take a long time to produce and the techniques of creating the complicated geometrical patterns are difficult to acquire.

The Tajiks, who live in the mountains north and east of Kabul, are of Iranian origin and speak a Persian dialect. There are many other minority groups also, such as the fair-skinned Nuristanis in the northeast—but no doubt remains that the Pathans are the masters in Afghanistan today. And there are many who will say that they deserve to be, for it was unquestionably the Pathans who organized successful resistance against the British in the two so-called Afghan Wars of the nineteenth century, when Queen Victoria's ministers, firmly entrenched in their great government houses in India, could not prevent their eyes from straying in other directions. Afghanistan is one of the very few countries of Asia that never, in modern history, became a European colony.

Pathans, warriors by nature, can still be seen wandering through the eastern mountains of Afghanistan with their rifles on their shoulders. Fierce as they may seem, however, their eyes are gentle, and they are among the friendliest people in the world. Once a foreigner learns their language and lives with them in one of their villages he will be treated as one of them and his life will be protected by his Pathan hosts at the risk of their own.

Pathans are also, as I have noted, the masters of Kabul—and of the government. Of the sixteen members of the cabinet, only two are non-Pathan, and most governors of provinces are Pathan. So, in a sense, it may be said that the future of Afghanistan depends on how well her present rulers succeed in diminishing their own power and involving all the other elements in the country in a truly cohesive government.

Like many other strategic cities of the world, Kabul is bisected by a river. This one makes its first appearance in literature in the Rig Veda and the Avesta, where it is spoken of as the Kubha, while Ptolemy calls it the Kophen. Nowadays it bears the same name as the city it waters and beautifies.

It may be thought of as Kabul's life blood—for without it, there could be no fertile valley, no city to enjoy over two millennia of occasionally fierce but always eventful history. As one wanders along the river banks, one sees women doing their laundry in its waters or filling pitchers; men kneeling and facing westward toward

17

AFGHANISTAN ✺

Mecca, to offer their prayers to the god Allah; men, wearing the baggy trousers their ancestors have worn for centuries, living beside the river. These are neither rulers nor bureaucrats: these are the people of Kabul who in the past created the history of their country and who now preserve its distinctive culture.

On the riverbank stands a large two-storied mosque, called the Masjid-i-Shah-do-Shamshira (The King of Two Swords), which commemorates, according to early muslim sources, the first entry of Islam into Kabul in the seventh century, for the mosque replaced a major Hindu temple that stood on the same site.

There are, of course, numerous other mosques in the city, the majority of whose population are Muslims of the Sunnite sect (although there is also a Shi'ite minority). The domes of the mosques, covered with Persian-blue tiles, and the sharp minarets beside them, tower everywhere over the rooftops. Remains of an ancient wall wind down to the river, and on all sides, beyond the city, stand low, white-brown mountains, with high distant peaks.

Babur was not the only great conqueror who lapsed into poetry when he thought about Kabul. Ahmad Khan, Durr-i-Durran ("the Pearl of Pearls"), as he came to be called, was in his early twenties when Nadir Shah, the Persian tyrant, whom he served and who had executed so many thousands, was himself executed. The Pearl of Pearls escaped from the camp, taking with him the Koh-i-Noor diamond and a number of Afghan troops. They eventually decided to declare their independence from Persia and, under the leadership of Durr-i-Durran, took the first steps toward the establishment of a unified and independent Afghanistan, the country of the Afghans. The year was 1747.

Years later, Ahmad Khan Durr-i-Durran wrote the following

poem in Pashto: "Many countries have I conquered, and I have renewed the memory of Sher Shah.* Yet never can I forget the many breathtaking orchards of my native land. And when I think of the rows and rows of jagged summits of her mountains, I forget even my throne in Delhi."

Kabul, however, is no different from any other city: if one wants to see what her citizens are really like, one must leave the gardens and the broad, tree-shaded avenues with their glittering new skyscrapers.

As soon as one does, in Kabul, one is likely to encounter her most persistent scent: that of mutton broiled in oil and mingled with the odor of rice fried with raisins and nuts. If we now follow our noses, we will soon reach a typical West Asian-style teahouse with a number of long benches on which people are sitting or squatting. The sooty ceiling is low, and the room is dimly lit. Water for the tea is boiling in a brass samovar.

After we have been welcomed by the proprietor, we are brought some dishes of broiled mutton and fried rice, along with a huge piece of thin bread called *nan*. This kind of bread is a staple throughout the entire area and has even spread as far as North Africa, although its name, naturally, differs in various countries. In the so-called Fertile Crescent area, ovens have been excavated dating back more than seven thousand years, suggesting that *nan* or its equivalent has been a staple food for the inhabitants of the region for at least that long.

Now comes the tea, either green or black, as in Japan. It seemed to me that Afghans are even fonder of tea than we are, and they

---

*Sher Shah was a Bengali Muslim of Afghan descent who conquered Hindustan after Babur's death and instituted a number of important civic reforms.

drink both green and black with lots of sugar. They will offer their guest a cup of tea on virtually any occasion, just as we do.

In villages, of course, with their closed societies, the teahouse plays a more important role than in a city like Kabul. No matter how small the village, so long as it has a bazaar, it will have a teahouse, where people come to meet one another, to play a popular game of marbles called *karom*, and to exchange the endless pieces of information—and misinformation—that village life seems to thrive on the world over. Marriage and money are, of course, among the chief topics of conversation—but in a country like Afghanistan, as our group was to discover, where water is more precious than land, the state of the wells takes precedence over all other subjects.

Then at last, sated by tidbits and tea, you leave the cool, dark room—and are suddenly smitten by the terrific glare of the Afghan sun. As soon as you are able, you look around and are struck by the brilliance of the ground red pepper which is being sold by weight in front of the teahouse.

You realize now how important strong color is to the Afghan. You remember the eye-shattering flamboyance of the printed material (much of it Japanese) that is for sale in the shops: it helps the Afghan to withstand the white glare of the sun and the red glare of the earth. A harsh environment requires a high degree of self-expression for survival. It is this very environment that had much to do, no doubt, with molding the personality and character of the Afghans.

The climate of the entire country, topographically diverse though it is, is a dry one, while variations in temperature are extremely wide. Shaped rather like an oak leaf, Afghanistan is actually a high plateau crossed from northeast to southwest by mountains varying in height from about ten to twenty thousand feet. Thus, it may, like ancient Gaul, be divided into three parts: the high mountain spurs in the center, with fertile valleys between; the vast plateau with oases to the north; and the deserts and semi-deserts toward the southwest, traversed by the River Helmand.

At the opposite end of the scale from my own country, Afghanistan is altogether landlocked. On the north, with the Oxus as a border, lie the Soviet Republics of Turkmenistan, Uzbekistan, and Tajikistan; west and south is Iran; to the east lies Pakistan.

The area of Afghanistan is approximately 250,000 square miles, about twice that of Japan, but its population is roughly the same as Tokyo. I say "roughly" because no comprehensive census has ever been made, and estimates vary widely—between ten and fifteen million. The nomad population has been estimated at about two million, but may be larger. One reason for this great disparity between land area and population is, of course, the fact that about half the country is composed of either high mountains or deserts—both unfit for human habitation. Thus, the greater part of the population is concentrated in oases of varying sizes bordering the wide rivers. Some of these oases are of great antiquity.

High and rugged mountains, uninhabitable deserts, green and fertile oases: these are the three components of Afghanistan's physical life.

The three mountain ranges that bisect the country from the Wakhan corridor in the northeast toward the southwest frontier are the Hindu Kush, a spur of the Himalayas which rises in the Little Pamir; the Koh-i-Baba, which continues the main ridge westward; and the Paropamisus Mountains, a series of lower ridges approaching the Iranian frontier.

AFGHANISTAN ※

The higher mountains are in the east, and the climate is correspondingly harsher; the rivers, fed by melting snow, are icy cold, and the only human habitation is at the southern tip of the valley, where shepherds may occasionally be seen tending their small flocks. The Wakhan corridor in the northeast, which is part of the Pamirs, the "roof of the world," is a long, narrow area that touches the frontiers of five countries: India, Pakistan, China, the Soviet Union, and Afghanistan. Wakhan Valley, which was formed during the Fourth Glacial Period, is characterized by rocky cliffs, some of which are over a thousand feet high.

Although the Hindu Kush broadens as it moves toward the west, the peaks of Central Afghanistan still average around fifteen thousand feet. In ancient Chinese accounts these awesome peaks were called simply "The Great Snowy Mountains," and the present name is said to mean "Hindu-Killer." Nonetheless, it was over the passes of the Hindu Kush, during permissible weather, that travelers and invaders alike entered the area now called Afghanistan, where some of them, if they survived the rigors of the journey, remained, while others continued on their way, for this range was an important corridor linking the basins of the Oxus in the north with those of the Indus in the east. In ancient times travelers used to wrap cloth around the hooves of the beasts in their caravan, to prevent their being mired in the snow; most merchants, nonetheless, expected to lose a part of their goods in this arduous and dangerous crossing. Now, during the summer months, the crossing may be made quite easily over the Salang Pass Super-highway.

The Hindu Kush may be said to end at the green valley of Bamiyan where the mountains then continue under the name of the Koh-i-Baba range, the "Grandfather Mountains." Lower than the

Hindu Kush, the range nonetheless possesses sizable peaks that average around twelve thousand feet. Climate is more temperate here, water more plentiful, sheep more abundant.

The Koh-i-Baba range was also an important "round-about" for the spread of civilization, for it serves as a watershed for four great rivers that flow through Afghanistan in four different directions: the Kabul, which heads eastward, pours into the Indus and the Indian subcontinent; the Hari Rud enters Iran to the west; the Helmand, flowing south, waters the semi-deserts of Sistan; while the Kunduz, converging with the Oxus, flows into Central Asia.

Serving as important avenues of communication, the rivers also act as natural boundaries. North of the Kabul, as it flows toward the Khybar Pass, is the district called the Eastern Province, which is surrounded by mountains and is blessed with an abundance of water. It is the only region that is slightly affected by the summer monsoon coming up from the plains of the Indus. The city of Kabul itself, rather dry, is almost seven thousand feet above sea level, while Jelalabad, which is less than two thousand feet high, is likely to be damp and sticky.

North of the Hindu Kush, the world is Central Asian. This northern plateau, which is separated from the Soviet Union by the Oxus, is the setting for the descent of the Mongol warriors, with their thin moustaches and their cloaks flying behind them as they galloped toward the west, threatening the European subcontinent itself. The scene was one of wide expanses of dry, stony soil, dotted by thousands of black specks of grazing sheep, with the fabled oases in the distance—for here lay the ancient Silk Route, the road that Marco Polo followed.

AFGHANISTAN ⚘

Here, trailing from oasis to oasis, came the long caravans bearing spices and silks and carpets and all the other treasures of the East for which the West was so hungry. The yellow dust that seeped through our bus perhaps plagued Marco Polo less, for he moved at a slower pace. Everyone and everything, people on top of the bus and in the bus, with their mountains of baggage, were covered with a film of yellow dust—but no one seemed to mind: they laughed and joked together as they ate sweet figs from Tash-Kurghan and hard *pistah* (pistachio) nuts. The road is being rebuilt, and eventually there will be a great highway here, but I doubt whether the passengers, even when they are traveling at a hundred miles an hour, will be very different from the way they are now—and they never should change, at least not from a romantic foreigner's point of view.

And it was here too, in this strategic northern corner of Afghanistan, that Alexander the Great brought his army and, after a hard struggle, succeeded in winning his way through to India. The Greek settlers that he left behind remained in possession of Bactria (modern Balkh) for some two centuries. Before this, Emperor Ashoka had sent missionaries into Afghanistan to preach Buddhism. Some centuries later, Buddhism flourished in the prosperous Kushan dynasty due to the patronage of the powerful ruler Kanishka. It was then that Buddhist painting and sculpture were influenced by the Greco-Roman art style, and the much admired art of the Gandhara School emerged. The remaining traces of this once great civilization can still be seen in Jelalabad, Bamiyan and Begram; many of the Gandhara masterpieces are now beautifully displayed in the Musée de Kaboul.

Turning now to the west, in our brief survey of Afghanistan's geography, we leave the foothills of the Paropamisus Range behind us and head for the Hari Rud River and the ancient and venerable city of Herat, near the Iranian frontier. The earth is barren and dry, reddish-yellow in color, dotted here and there with dwarfed and clearly undernourished trees: these are the source of those *pistah* nuts that the passengers on the Silk Route bus were eating. I was reminded of a poem by Sa'adi, a famous poet from Shiraz: "I thought of him as filled tightly with a hard inner core like a *pistah* nut, but found him to be but an onion, wearing skin after skin."

Now the Iranian world begins to move into clearer focus, and as we approach Herat, the language itself takes on a more sharply Iranian flavor. Although Persian, along with Pashto, is one of the two official languages of the country, the Persian spoken in Afghanistan is very different from that heard in the vicinity of Tehran.

Herat has never been entirely destroyed by invading conquerors and today is still green and a thriving city watered by the Hari Rud. On both sides of its wide paved streets stand rows of tall conifers, and there are famous monuments aplenty: mosques, mausoleums, and minarets. The old tiles of Herat's best-known building, the Masjid-i-Jami (the Friday, or Congregational, Mosque), preserve their brilliant blue after all these hundreds of years—perhaps, at least in part, because the annual precipitation here is only about eight inches.

In the south is the vast arid plain of Sistan and Registan, through which flows the great Helmand River. Here there is almost no rainfall whatsoever the year round, the sun beats mercilessly down day after day on the wasteland, and the traveler sees almost nothing to delight or relieve his burning eyes: only a super-highway running straight and apparently endlessly through the yellowish-white plain.

AFGHANISTAN ✻

To protect ourselves against the unbearably hot winds, we wrapped ourselves up thoroughly and with gloved hands wound towels around our faces. We had a polyvinyl tank of water, from which we kept taking sips—even though in a very short while the water was disagreeably hot. We were plagued by mirages: white sea coasts and green pine trees appeared and disappeared.

Then, like another mirage, there rose in the midst of the desert the ruins of a castle town stretching some three miles in length. But this was no mirage—this was Lashkargah, the former winter capital of the Ghaznavid dynasty. There are remains of thick mud walls to be seen, and small, labyrinthine rooms, with ornate carvings in niches—but it was hard in this burning silence to reconstruct the din and bustle that must once have animated this ancient site.

For more than five thousand years this desert has been a major crossroads of civilization. Not far from Kandahar is a prehistoric site where some beautiful painted pottery has been found that— I believe—may be intimately associated with the painted-pottery cultures of both Sistan in Iran and the Baluchistan-Indus region in India.

Soon, perhaps, the desert will be reclaimed again. The Helmand River Project, the Afghanistan counterpart of the Tennessee Valley Project, undertaken with American aid, is constructing modern factories and office buildings as well as private houses adjacent to the great castle town of the Ghazni dynasty, and in the air-conditioned hotel there is a large swimming pool filled with emerald green water. Eventually, by means of a complex system of irrigation and hydroelectric plants, it is hoped that this wasteland will supply the people of Afghanistan with some of the agricultural products they still so sorely lack. Already, the basin of the Arghandab River has been successfully developed into a rich farming area through a "siphon system" of irrigation, with river waters brought into canals through pipelines—but the project itself has many problems, which I shall mention later.

One way of gaining insight into the character of a foreign people is to have a look at the games they play. The most popular sport of the people of Afghanistan is *buz-kashi*, although it is played only on national holidays and important occasions like the King's birthday. The reader will soon see why it could hardly be played much more often.

Each team consists of anywhere between ten and a thousand horsemen, almost always of the same tribe. The "ball," so to speak, is a beheaded goat disemboweled and filled with sand and placed in a hole in the middle of a wide plain. The object of the game is to get the carcass out of the hole and carry it around the "goal-posts," which may be several kilometers away, then back to the original site.

Once the animal has been removed from the hole, it becomes, naturally, the object of a fierce struggle as members of the opposing team try to snatch it from the rider who presently has it. Horses are specially trained not only for speed and endurance but also to assist the rider by kneeling on signal so that he may have a better chance to snatch the decapitated beast. A horse may even seize it in his teeth for his rider to recover and carry. The "ball," obviously, changes hands numerous times during the game.

Each rider carries a stout leather whip with which he not only goads on his horse but may also slash at the faces of opponents. A rider who falls is likely to be mangled, and broken ribs are not uncommon. On the other hand, the injured are treated like heroes

27

by their own tribe. I once heard a *buz-kashi* rider say, as he stroked his moustache, that it was not the broken leg he had suffered in the game that bothered him, but the fact that he would no longer be able to play. Had he not been a Pathan, I would have said that the gleam in his eye might have been a tear.

How, the reader might ask, could such a people ever be conquered? The fact is, of course, that until the eighteenth century Afghanistan was not a nation but a geographical area, and even so, no conqueror, of whom there were many, was able to hold the area for very long. In a very real sense, Afghanistan was the crossroads of the world—and a crossroads is always likely to be a disputed area. At least five world-shaking empires have risen here, and it was a strategic part of the pathway between East and West long before there was a difference between them. If, as seems likely, civilization "began" somewhere near the eastern shore of the Mediterranean, then it soon started to spread in all directions—and it was the same civilization. To me it seems strange to speak of Oriental history as opposed to Occidental history: after all, the so-called "continents" of Europe and Asia are in reality one. We should remember, too, that in Eurasian history Afghanistan often played the role of a "round-about."

The chief attraction that Afghanistan held for the would-be conqueror was, of course, its strategic location between East and West, between the Oxus and the Indus. It is interesting to note that much the same route across present-day Afghanistan was traversed by Alexander the Great in the fourth century B.C., by the Chinese priest Hsüan-tsang in the seventh century A.D., and by the fourteenth-century Moroccan, Ibn Battuta. The latter two wrote books about their travels which make fascinating reading; even more interesting might have been Alexander's reminiscences had he lived to a ripe old age and found the time to write them.

It ought to be noted, further, that considerable parts of this same road are now being used in twentieth-century Afghanistan as national highways. Although the road from Kandahar to Farah, a roundabout route that Alexander used, does not today form part of it, there is now a super-highway running directly from Kabul to Herat via Kandahar, over which one may drive at a hundred miles an hour without feeling one is asking too much of the road's surface. Similarly, there is a super-highway north from Kabul into Central Asia, via Kunduz, of which several miles cross the Hindu Kush through the Salang Tunnel. In July the highway is shaded by large, ancient mulberry trees laden with ripe and luscious clusters of berries. The southern road to Kandahar was completed with American aid, while that to the north had Soviet assistance. Afghanistan, thus, still lies in a strategic position between East and West. Let us hope it continues to be a crossroads of civilization—and not its battleground, or graveyard.

"I entered the Great Snowy Mountains," wrote Hsüan-tsang in the year 632, "from the southeast. Valleys are deep and summits are dangerous. Here the wind is very strong, the snow piles high, and the temperature is below freezing even in summer. The valleys themselves are filled with snow, which makes passage extremely difficult. In addition, roving bands wait to pounce upon the traveler, killing and robbing him. After covering six hundred *li*, (about one hundred miles) I finally arrived at Bamiyan."

The road to Bamiyan that the Buddhist priest took, as he describes it in his book, *Travels in Western Countries*, has been superseded by a modern highway, over which pass speeding cars, as well as veiled

AFGHANISTAN 业

nomad women leading heavily-laden donkeys. Being greedy, we went one way and came back the other. The trip, on either route, usually takes about six or seven hours, but took us more than ten, as we often stopped along the way to chat with friendly Afghans.

Traversing the tree-lined road, we reached the valley around dusk to be confronted suddenly by a colossal Buddha carved in the cliff to our right. Although the smaller of two giant Buddhas, it was 120 feet high. The technique used here was roughly as follows: the figure was carved, then cloaked in a mixture of mud and straw, and finally painted. Traces of blue may still be seen.

The hands are gone and the face has been mutilated, as is the case with almost every face, painted or sculptured, in the whole Bamiyan complex. The reason of course is obvious. In taking over the monotheism of the Jews, the Muslims also took over their abhorrence of idols—but whereas the Jews were generally content to let other peoples worship such gods as they chose, the Muslims, fired by their faith, and in the throes of fervent efforts to create an international cultural unit in the name of Allah, often felt obliged to destroy the idols they encountered. Much priceless art was destroyed in the process, but, of course, trivial when compared with the savage vandalism of our atomic-age wars.

Around the giant figure were numerous caves dug into the cliff; the gaping black holes reminded me of an enormous beehive. There are corridors and steps connecting the caves, which continue for several miles. People say there are in all some twenty thousand caves, but I wondered if anyone had ever tried to count them. The larger Buddha—175 feet tall—is on the western side of the cliff, and this too is faceless and armless. Temples and dwelling-quarters for the priests were concentrated around the two figures.

"There are more than ten monasteries and more than a thousand priests," wrote Hsüan-tsang. Today the entire valley has only a thousand inhabitants. The Chinese pilgrim says also that the face of the giant Buddha was covered with gold and decorated with precious gems "that dazzle the eye." There are remains of painting and sculpture to be seen also on the variously shaped ceilings of the caves; some are oblong, some cylindrical, triangular, or dome-shaped.

This astonishing cultural activity was previously thought to have begun in the third century, while the Kushans were still in power. But the Buddhas, colossal as they are, seem rather heavy when compared with the Gandharan Buddhist statues of the Kushan dynasty and bear a closer resemblance to statues created during the Gupta dynasty in India (fourth to fifth century). The wall paintings also are reminiscent of those to be seen in the caves of Ajanta, put up during the flowering of the Gupta culture, or of the Sassanids (third to seventh century), while some architectural forms seem close to those found in Syria and other east Mediterranean countries. For these—and other reasons that space does not permit me to list here—I would date the Buddhist cultural activities of Bamiyan somewhere between the fourth and seventh centuries.

But more important than the date of production, it seems to me, is the fact that the creators of this culture not only adapted diverse elements from many parts of the world and harmonized them, but achieved their own unique and homogeneous culture. The relics at Bamiyan are not mere by-products of the history that was unrolling on the road between India and Persia—they are in themselves an expression of a separate and distinct culture.

31

AFGHANISTAN ☙

The Prophet Mohammed died at Medina in 632, and it seems reasonable to suppose that there were Arab propagandists in Kandahar no later than the year 700. Yet when a Buddhist monk visited the place in the first half of the ninth century he found it much the same as it had been—with a devout Buddhist king, priesthood, and people. Tenth century accounts also indicate that Buddhism still flourished in Bamiyan. The survival of this Buddhist culture through several centuries indicates that the Arabs could be lenient toward another religion. In fact, by this time the chief aim of the Arabs in conquering other regions was not necessarily to impose their faith on the people or to destroy their socio-cultural systems, but to collect tributes from Buddhist communities. The well-known expression, "the Koran or the sword" is a Western-inspired exaggeration of the religious zeal of the Muslims. We do not know how this astounding Buddhist culture died out, but there is no evidence whatever that its extinction was due to Arab fanaticism. Possibly, there may have been an upheaval in the social or economic conditions that caused its final disintegration.

By the following century, during the Ghaznavid dynasty, Islam was established throughout Afghanistan, including Bamiyan, which now became involved in the intrigues of various Islamic dynasties until, in 1222, Genghis Khan sent his grandson to lay seige to the nearby fortress of Shahr-i-Zohak. The boy was killed during the battle, and Genghis Khan, enraged, vowed to put to death every living thing within the valley—even children still in their mothers' wombs. On a hill opposite the caves of Bamiyan stand the crumbling ruins of another city devastated by the Mongol hordes; it came to be known as Shahr-i-Gholghola, "the City of Noise," the noise being the shrieks of the dying citizens.

With the passing of the years, nomad tribes came into the valley, and soon some of them began to settle down in now abandoned Buddhist cells or build permanent houses and till the fertile soil. Their descendants were overwhelmingly kind to us. They not only helped us carry our heavy photographic equipment but even, at one point, when we had to ford a chest-high river, tried to carry us. We thanked them, but said that if they could forge across the river, so could we. They would guide us to the ruins, then silently disappear before we had a chance to offer them something for their help. The proprietor of a teahouse took care to see that he had a stock of fresh eggs to prepare for us each morning we were there. A shoemaker made rubber slippers for us out of old tires. The owner of a bicycle shop taught us the local dances.

These were all members of the Hazara tribe, whose social status, as I noted earlier, is not very high in Afghanistan, one of the reasons being that they are Muslims of the Shi'ite sect, while the majority of Afghans are Sunnites. Since Shi'ites adhere not to Abu Bakr, the first caliph, but rather to the fourth caliph, 'Ali, Mohammed's cousin and son-in-law, legends about 'Ali are numerous among the Hazaras in the valley of Bamiyan. Some say there are over a thousand such legends. One that is particularly prevalent concerns the slaying of a dragon, some five miles west of the Buddhist relics—a particularly vicious dragon who demanded, for his daily subsistence, six hundred pounds of food, two camels, and a young girl. But the day came when, along with his food, he found a warrior waiting for him, sword in hand. The warrior was 'Ali, the dragon was slain and may still be seen, in petrified form, with little rushes of spring water from his eyes that are said to be his tears. The villagers still tell these stories to their children, and thus the ancient legends live on, also functioning as a unifying factor for their social solidarity against other dominant tribes.

The Bamiyan Valley Hazaras still use the caves as dwelling-places, though the government has forbidden them to make use of the ancient cells. Soot from their fires has regrettably damaged some of the wall paintings, but soot is as much the record of a living and vital humanity as painting is—although, to be sure, the vitality of a people who once created a great tribal kingdom is no longer to be seen here today. No animosity greeted our approach, only a group begging us to treat the eyes of an old woman who was suffering from a severe case of trachoma.

Back in Kabul, it was now time to begin preparations for our month's stay in a village. We had first to secure permission from both the Ministry of Foreign Affairs and the Ministry of the Interior; then we called on three other ministries—those of Education, Agriculture, and Information—to request their cooperation as well.

I should explain here, as we explained to the various government officials who aided us, that our group, composed of students of agriculture and engineering, was interested above all in observing at first hand the mechanics of a *karez*, that age-old system of finding, storing, and utilizing water which is to be seen all over Central and West Asia and even in North Africa. As with so many of man's most useful inventions, the origins of the *karez* are obscure, but apparently it existed in Persia at least twenty-five hundred years ago. Today there are said to be between twenty and thirty thousand *karez* in operation in Iran. The number currently in use in Afghanistan is even more uncertain, for no comprehensive survey of water-rights has ever been made, nor is there any map in existence showing the approximate number or location of these underground water channels.

Our group had its first sight of a *karez* on board the Aryana Afghan plane that brought us from New Delhi to Kabul. There is not much to be seen—a long row of earth mounds that could, conceivably, be ant-hills—till you reach the end product of this row of mounds: a bright patch of green, like an island in the surrounding desert, and a village that feeds on the green. Without the *karez* there could be neither vegetation nor people to make use of it. In these arid regions, far from rivers, if you dig a well, you've got to go hundreds of feet down on the chance of striking water, and that may turn out to be salt water. But with a *karez*, as indicated in the accompanying diagram, borings for underground water are first made at relatively shallow places in the foothills of a mountain, and the water is conducted to the earth's surface through an inclined underground channel. The mounds are essential to the actual digging of the channel and also to subsequent cleaning operations. The *karez* is the village's only source of water—a man-made oasis in the vast Asian deserts.

Having secured the necessary permission, we now had to determine what village could house us for a month and we had to be sure that the *karez* system in use in the village was an appropriate size for the purposes of our study. With these two problems in mind, we called on a public health research worker named Mr. Abdul Mohammed, whose elder brother had studied in Japan and who welcomed us like old friends.

He also turned out to be extremely helfpul to us, and it was through him that we solved our problems. Without his untiring help, we might not have succeeded in carrying out our village study. Like many high-ranking government officials in Kabul, Mr. Abdul's ancestors belonged to the land-owning class, and he himself came from a village about twenty-five miles south of Kabul on the Logar plateau. There were, he said, several villages in the neighborhood that would satisfy our conditions, pointing out that it would be more convenient for us not to be far from Kabul, so that we could be in touch with government agencies when necessary.

Mr. Abdul very kindly offered to introduce us to the magistrate of the district, who was a friend of his, as well as to his own cousin, a big land-owner who was building a new house where Mr. Abdul believed we could have rooms. An added inducement, as he pointed out, was the fact that his own village obtained water from the Logar River; thus we would be able to compare this type of irrigation with a *karez* system.

With Mr. Abdul guiding us, we started out one morning in our rented jeep for the Logar. Our road went past the Bala Hissar, perhaps the most significant of all Kabul's ancient monuments, a giant fortress and citadel atop a hill. At present a military academy, it is closed to tourists, but plans are afoot to turn it into a museum. And indeed it should be, for it is the heart of Kabul, and its history is Kabul's history. Up until quite recently, when Kabul began to expand, it commanded the entire city, and Kabul's famous walls, twelve feet thick, began at Bala Hissar. Construction on the walls was started, it is generally assumed, in the fifth century and continued for thirteen hundred years.

The citadel passed, as Kabul did, from conqueror to conqueror, and while it was in the hands of Babur, he wrote: "It is remarkably high and well-placed, looking over a large lake and three meadows that are extremely beautiful when they are in flower."

36

To right and left, that morning as we passed, we could see fields of yellowing wheat and wide green pastures. Black felt tents, made out of sheep's wool, were dwellings of the nomad shepherds. We saw other tents also, under the mulberry trees, very simple tents made of cotton. On our left we passed a light green irrigation canal that drew its water from the Logar. Poplars (valuable building material in a land that lacks timber) grew on both sides of the canal. We asked how much a sapling cost and were told—to our surprise—that the price was about two hundred afghani ($10 at the official rate). A very high price, we thought, for such a thin piece of wood.

After continuing a bit further, we turned to the left and soon were out of sight of the Logar River. We entered a vast, fan-shaped expanse of dry, unfertile plain covered with unattractive-looking whitish earth and surrounded by mountains. Here and there we saw dried-up river beds and in the far distance, and at the foothills of the mountains, patches of green. It was one of these patches of green that was to be our home for the next month, for it was they who were dependent on a *karez* economy. Once again I felt a deep thrill of respect for man, who digs at the foothills of a mountain, strikes underground water, and transforms a desert into a green and fertile place.

As we continued on toward the village that Mr. Abdul had in mind, we saw that the ant-hill mounds extended over a couple of miles. We were unable to look inside the wells because most of the holes in the tiny mounds were covered over to keep out the crumbling earth. The first well was probably about a hundred feet deep, but approaching the village the wells grew shallower.

Just before we entered the village, we paused to admire the

outlet for the wells, from which water gushed into an open canal.
What an invigorating sight this was in the midst of an uninhabitable
desert! Fish—black shadows in the bright sunlight—darted away
as we approached. The water is now collected into a pond, from
which it is conducted into the village, which lies secure behind
its thick mud walls. From here the water flows into the fields on
which the village feeds (see p. 50). The name of the village,
by the way, was Mirza Khel. Literally, "khel" means "the descent
of." Although the word can be applied to a group as large as a
"tribe," it usually denotes a localized community with intricate
kinship relations among its members. Originally, "Mirza" meant
"princely person," but it now can mean a clerk or government
official, and the fact is that most of the land-owners of the village
were working at their jobs in Kabul a large part of the time. I shall
have more to say about this point in a moment.

Digging vertically through dry, crumbling earth is, of course,
a job for an expert, and villagers call in men called *karez-kans*,
who seem to know almost instinctively where to dig for underground water. Usually they work in teams of four, under a leader
called the *salar*. Their average daily wage is four hundred afghani
($20), of which the *salar* takes half. Considering that the salary of a
fairly high-ranking government official is between three and four
thousand afghani a month ($150-200), it is obvious that *karez-
kans* are well paid—though it must be noted that the risk of danger
is ever-present.

It takes from two to three years to complete the construction of a
karez water-system—so it is clearly impossible for a single farmer
or land-owner to underwrite the whole expense. What almost
always happens is that several men band together to employ *karez-*

kans to build the water system, and this group accordingly owns all the rights to the water on which the village depends. The amount of land a man possesses is directly dependent on how much water he has a right to. The muslim law guarantees him land commensurate with the water that he "owns."

However, through the fickleness of time, chance, and fortune, it has come about that there are land-owners with insufficient water or even with no water at all. If such a man is to use his land, then, he is going to have to buy water. For one hour of water supplied over a ten-day period, in the cycle he will have to pay around a hundred and fifty pounds of grain in the course of the year.

Another class of villager is the tenant farmer, who possesses but one of the five requisites of agriculture: his own labor. The other four—land, water, seed, and livestock and farm implements—he lacks. Thus the land-owner who supplies them usually takes two-thirds, or sometimes even four-fifths, of the tenant farmer's entire harvest. Or the tenant farmer may agree to pay the land-owner a fixed amount—say, five hundred pounds of grain per year—no matter what his harvest may be. Under the tenant system based on division of profit, the land-owner may decide what the crop is to be; under the tenant system based on fixed amount, the farmer is free to grow whatever crop he chooses so long as he abides by the contract he has made with the land-owner. In either case, the tenant farmer is severely restricted and hardly likely to grow rich, while the land and water-owner, despite his big investment in a *karez* usually reaps a tremendous profit.

In our village there were a total of eleven land-owners, who might, with equal accuracy, be described as water-lords, and they jointly owned the Mirza Khel Karez. Most of them were government officials who lived and worked in Kabul, leaving the village work to hired laborers and tenant farmers. The Mirza Khel landlords were fortunate in the village being so near Kabul that they could make frequent visits to keep an eye on their property—land and water and the products of the two.

The landlords were fortunate also in the fact that they received salaries in Kabul, which enabled them to lend money to their tenant farmers. Interest is prohibited under muslim law, but the landlords found a way to circumvent the prohibition effectively. Let us say a tenant farmer's share of the autumn harvest was insufficient to last him and his valley through the winter. He goes to his landlord, accordingly, and borrows a hundred pounds of grain, the price of which is high because the harvest season is past. Perhaps he promises to pay five hundred afghani for the hundred pounds of grain. At the time of the next harvest, the land-owner demands to be repaid his five hundred afghani of grain. The price being down, the tenant farmer may now have to return to the land-owner even two hundred pounds of grain to replace the hundred he borrowed several months past. However, since the landlord has received no interest, he has not broken muslim law. And the tenant farmer has learned to keep his mouth shut.

Nevertheless, he seemingly does not consider his life to be hard or dreary; on the contrary, he seems to enjoy it far more than people do in a Japanese farming community today. Once I asked one of Mirza Khel's tenant farmers what he thought of the land-owners. His face broke into a smile. "They work very hard," he replied. "The other day they visited us while we were harvesting the wheat, and they said, 'Come on, brothers, take an hour off and have some tea. You're working too hard. But first let's finish up this patch here.'"

One of the villagers who was most attentive to us, a kind and affable man, worked as a farmhand for Haji Sahib, the chief landowner of the village and a cousin of our friend Abdul. As his name indicated, Haji Sahib had made the pilgrimage to Mecca.

The farmhand was so scrawny that we nicknamed him "Ostoghan," which might be translated as Mr. Bones. Now, Mr. Bones had, at that time, been working for Sir Pilgrim for over seven years, signing a contract to work from the spring planting period through the autumn harvest: a total of nine months. During the winter, he usually lived in Haji Sahib's house, looking after the livestock and performing various chores that needed to be done. Mr. Bones was treated very much like one of the family.

The relationship continued to be affable despite the fact that Mr. Bones had asked to be promoted to the status of tenant farmer, and the request had been refused. Haji Sahib told him that, as a farmhand, he was guaranteed food and shelter, though his life in many ways was like that of a slave; as a tenant farmer, he would be guaranteed nothing, only because he would have his "freedom." "Which do you think is better off?" asked Mr. Abdul, with a meaningful smile, as we stood together by the window one day. Mr. Bones, in his usual jovial mood, was piling a huge bale of wheat onto a donkey's back, to be carried to the threshing-floor, where oxen took over.

I was hard put to know what reply to make, and perhaps Mr. Abdul expected none. Could I explain that, though the farming communities we had examined seemed peaceful enough, I had glimpsed some chinks in the hitherto solid feudal system? Nonetheless, the farmers do not seem unhappy or depressed. Farmers don't usually do much smiling—with the exception of those I saw in Afghanistan. Their cheerfulness is partly a technique for living happily under constant oppression, and partly a display of their native vitality, which has enabled them to wring a livelihood out of the arid and unfriendly desert.*

It is interesting to compare Afghanistan's farmers with her nomad tribesmen. The confrontation between the two groups has shaped the history of many a country, but here in Afghanistan the two groups have lived for centuries in a kind of symbiosis. The farmers depended on the nomads for culture and trade, meanwhile supplying a stable economic foundation. But with the establishment of a cash-economy and with the gradual restriction of grazing ground, the nomad has come to depend on the farmer more and more. Where once, long ago, the nomads treated the sedentary farmers with contempt and subjected them to periodic plunder, they have now begun to take up the sedentary life themselves. Some hire themselves out as farmhands at meager salaries.

But here is an interesting case. In one village near Mirza Khel Karez, nomadic tribesmen had purchased two-fifths of the water-rights of a *karez*—at a price of 170,000 afghanis ($8,500)—and half the tribal families now cultivated two-fifths of the village land. The other half of the tribe still grazed their herds in the warm plains of the Eastern Province during the winter and in the central mountains during the summer, following their age-old transhumance pattern.

The great nomadic tribes of Afghanistan are still in possession of huge herds of sheep and goats, and they continue to wield political as well as economic power—but the increasing modernization of the country tends to curtail nomad power. The object of the Helmand River Project, which is being accomplished with American aid, is to provide land and water for approximately eight hun-

---

*A full report of the village study is now being prepared for publication.

dred thousand nomadic tribesmen and their families—but I wonder whether the tribesmen themselves are in favor of the plan.

Even government officials resent the too-modernized semi-American town set down in the middle of their harsh desert. If one ignores the existing culture of these people and attempts to impose a second with a neatly packaged "aid" based on the standards of a different culture, one will not only lose their gratitude and goodwill, but will spoil and corrupt their lives. Thus, far more important, it seems to me, is to find some way to renew the vitality this ancient people once possessed—the vitality that enabled them to survive and prosper under appallingly hard conditions. The government of the country is currently placing its main emphasis on education and on irrigation and sanitation in its attempt to develop stable farming communities. I believe that if the project is to succeed, the government will also have to find some way to foster the ancient virtues of independence and self-reliance.

The future, due to steady modernization, promises much for the Afghans. A new, progressive constitution was promulgated in 1964, and since 1967 the Third Five-Year Plan has been in effect. On Afghanistan's Independence Day, throughout the country, the variety of products made possible by modernization programs is displayed. With the completion of the Salang Pass Highway, which links the northern and the southern regions of Afghanistan, and the opening of the new international airport in Kandahar, Afghanistan may once again become an important crossroads of civilization. After our return to Japan, one of the members of our group said that he would be very much interested to see Afghanistan in another twenty years. Another said that he wouldn't mind turning around and going back right then!

Cultural Chronology (by J. Hara)

Year	Cultural History	Period
4000	Painted pottery: Mundigak, Nadiali Rig Veda	PREHISTORIC
2000	First wave of Aryan migration; horses used for riding	
1000	Second wave of Aryan migration; life of the prophet Zoroaster	MEDIAN KINGDOM
500	521–485 Reign and conquest of Darius I divides country into Gandhara and Bactria	ACHAEMENID DYNASTY
	ca. 566–486 Life of Gautama Buddha	
300	330 Alexander the Great in Aryana (ancient Afghanistan)	ALEXANDRIAN DYNASTY / MAURYA DYNASTY
	273 Enthronement of King Ashoka and consequent spread of Buddhism	SELEUCID DYNASTY
200	250 Kingdom of Bactria becomes independent and Greek Bactrian culture flourishes	BACTRIAN KINGDOM
	183 Demetrius conquers Punjab and southern Afghanistan; origination of King Melinda's Buddhist doctrines	
	130 Saka invade Bactria; Yüeh-chih in northern Afghanistan; Chang Ch'ien's expedition sent by Han emperor	PARTHIANS — SAKA YÜEH-CHIH
B.C. A.D. 100	45 Kadphises founds Kushan dynasty in northern Afghanistan	KUSHAN DYNASTY
200	144 King Kanishka enthroned and Buddhism reaches high peak; Gandhara art emerges	
	241 Invasion of Shadpur I; Sassanian wall paintings at Bamiyan; Stupa arts at Hadda; origination of Manichaeism	SASSANID DYNASTY / SMALL KUSHAN DYNASTY
400	460 Invasion by "White Huns" (Ephthalites)	EPHTHALITE
500	565 Ephthalites defeated by Turks	SASSANID DYNASTY
600	663 Arab domination of Balkh	
800	814–973 Taharid dynasty in Khorasan	TAHARID DYNASTY
	827 Korean Monk Hui-ch'ao visits Bamiyan	SAFFARID DYNASTY
	870 Kabul and Bamiyan under Arab sway	
900	962 Ghaznavid dynasty founded at Ghazni; city becomes a great cultural center	SAMANID DYSASTY
	993 Rule of Sultan Mahmud	

	Year	Event	Dynasty
1000	1006	Life of Khwaja Ansari, poet and philosopher	GHAZNAVID DYNASTY
1100	1148	Ghoris supplant Turkish rulers of Ghazni; Indo-Islamic culture flourishes; Masjid-i-Jami constructed in Herat	KHORASM / GHORI DYNASTY
1200			
	1220	Invasion by Genghis Khan; destruction of Herat, Balkh, Bamiyan, Ghazni, and of irrigation systems	MONGOL EMPIRE
	1258	Il-khanid Kingdom	IL-KHANID KINGDOM
1300	1300	Pathans march to Hindu Kush; travels of Marco Polo	
	1370	Timur (Tamerlane) becomes king at Balkh; travels of Ibn Battuta	TIMURID DYNASTY
1400	1404	Islamic culture flourishes at Herat during Timurid dynasty established by Shah Rukh	
1500	1505	Babur captures Kabul	SAFAVID DYNASTY / MUGHAL DYNASTY
	1525	Mughals conquer India	
1600	1625	Kandahar occupied by the Safavids	
1700	1708	Mir Wais Hotoki liberates western Afghanistan from Safavids; Afghan domination in Persia	
	1722	Safavid rule ended by Afghans, but Afghan expansion halted by Khorasamiani conqueror Nadir Afshar	
	1744	Ahmad Shah lays foundation of modern Afghanistan	
1800	1834	Amir Dost Muhammad Khan establishes present kingdom; Jamal-ud-Din, Muslim philosopher	DURRANI DYNASTY
	1838	First Afghan War (–1842)	BARAKZAI DYNASTY
	1878	Second Afghan War (–1881)	
	1893	Establishment of Durand line	
1900	1919	Third Afghan War; Western way of life introduced due to enlightened rule of King Amanullah	
	1929	Revolt of Baiha-i-Saqa put down by Nadir Shah who ascends throne as constitutional monarch	
	1933	H. M. Mohammad Zahir Shah ascends throne	
	1956	First Five-Year Plan	
	1964	Promulgation of new constitution	

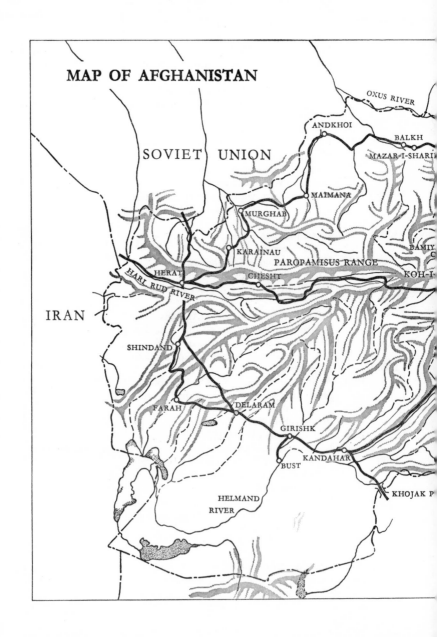

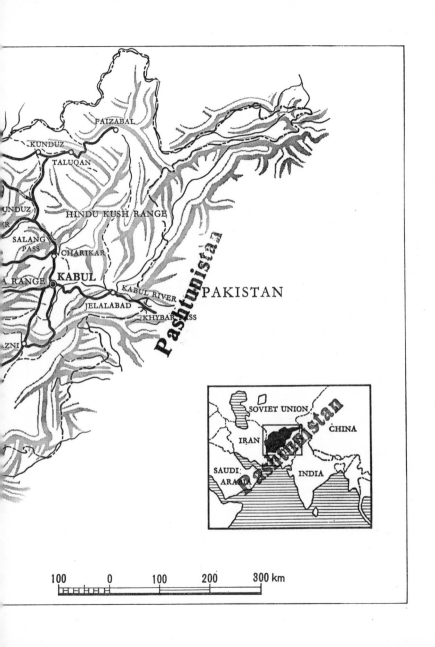

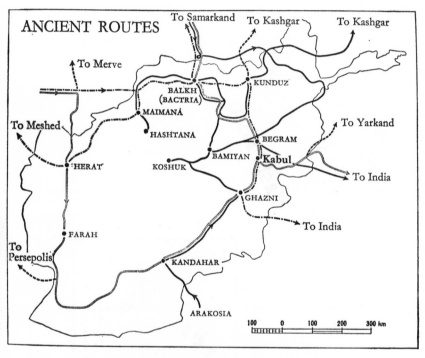

ANCIENT ROUTES

To Samarkand To Kashgar To Kashgar

To Merve

To Meshed

BALKH
(BACTRIA)

KUNDUZ

MAIMANÁ

HASHTANA

BEGRAM

To Yarkand

BAMIYAN Kabul

KOSHUK

HERAT

To India

GHAZNI

To India

FARAH

To
Persepolis

KANDAHAR

ARAKOSIA

100   0   100   200   300 km

——— ROUTE OF ALEXANDER THE GREAT (*fourth century B.C.*)

——— ROUTE OF HSÜAN-TSING (*seventh century*)

—·—·— ROUTE OF IBN BATTUTA (*fourteenth century*)

—·—·— OTHER TRADITIONAL COMMERCIAL ROUTES

CROSS SECTION OF A KAREZ

(The diagram below is the ground plan of the above cross-section)

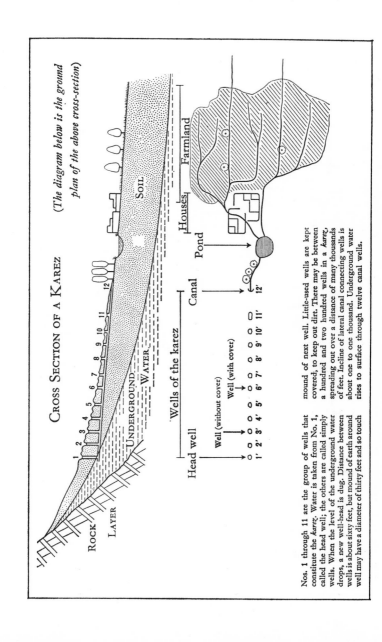

Nos. 1 through 11 are the group of wells that constitute the *karez*. Water is taken from No. 1, called the head well; the others are called simply wells. When the level of the underground water drops, a new well-head is dug. Distance between wells is about sixty feet, but mound of earth around well may have a diameter of thirty feet and so touch mound of next well. Little-used wells are kept covered, to keep out dirt. There may be between a hundred and two hundred wells in a *karez*, spreading out over a distance of many thousands of feet. Incline of lateral canal connecting wells is about one to one thousand. Underground water rises to surface through twelve canal wells.

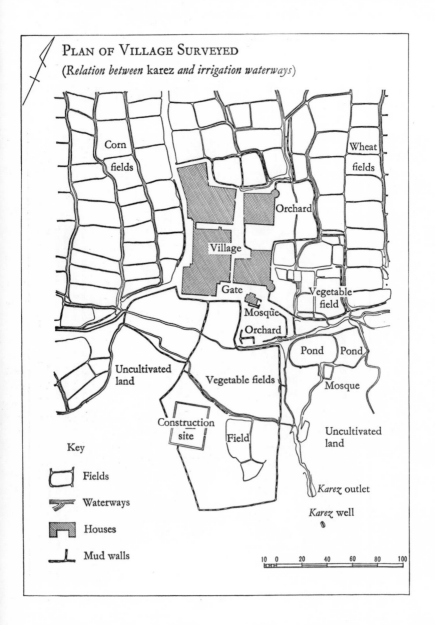

PLAN OF VILLAGE SURVEYED
(*Relation between* karez *and irrigation waterways*)

Corn fields

Wheat fields

Orchard

Village

Gate

Mosque

Orchard

Vegetable field

Pond   Pond

Mosque

Uncultivated land

Vegetable fields

Uncultivated land

Construction site

Field

Karez outlet

Karez well

Key

Fields

Waterways

Houses

Mud walls

10 0   20   40   60   80   100

5. *Tomb of 'Ali,* fourth caliph after Mohammed, is especially sacred to the Shi'ites, although the Blue Mosque to house it (entrance shown below) was built by the rival Sunnites—probably to stir up business on the ancient trade route.

6. *Patterned hillside (see overleaf)* in one of the vast arid regions of Afghanistan; millions of herded beasts must have crossed this desert slope in the past five or six thousand years, on their way to greener pastures. ▶

7. *Children* are likely to stare at foreigners here as they do elsewhere in the world; at first, walls of village houses seem inhospitable, but inside, a visitor finds a generous welcome.

8. *Oldest man* in the group is in the front as these devout Muslims touch their foreheads to the ground; prayers are offered five times a day.

10. *At roadside bazaars,* rug-vendors frequently have their wares draped picturesquely over their shoulders; the older gentleman at the left seems to be on the point of purchase.

9. *Long-distance bus* has replaced the camel, the donkey, and the horse as the standard means of transport between one remote spot in Afghanistan and another: it is a caravan in itself.

11. *After the harvest,* nomads and farmers alike turn their livestock loose on the formerly green fields to glean what they can of wheat or corn.

12. *Unai Pass* (10,330 feet) through the Koh-i-Baba range is seldom used by travelers from Kabul to Bamiyan nowadays, but here a nomad family spurns the modern highway.

13. *Siah-koh Highway* winds its tortuous way through the mountains between Kabul and Jelalabad, then continues on through the Khybar Pass to Pakistan.

14. *Bibicol and Noeda,* the two girls on the right, are sisters; the other girl is their cousin; and all three are daughters of landowners; little Bibicol is dressed for a holiday, while the older girls are wearing their school uniforms.

15. *Three teachers* from a girls' high school, unveiled and—so it would seem—uninhibited by the antique customs that so often make the life of a muslim woman monotonous and dreary.

16. *Backstreet* of a bazaar in Kabul, where the various ethnic groups of Afghanistan mingle and trade: the front of a bazaar is likely to be a glittering world of light, its backstreets a realm of shadows.

17. *Second-hand clothes market,* where
goods collected from charity bazaars
in America and elsewhere are offered
to Afghans: a jacket is likely to sell for
less than a dollar, a suit of the best
quality for less than ten.

18. *Rug-vendors* offering their wares: an Afghan could tell you, by looking at the colors and the designs, in just what part of the country the rugs were made.

19. *Male Afghans,* like all Muslims, must wear some sort of head-covering; these caps, threaded with gold and beaded, also betray their origin to the knowing.

20. *Karakul skins*—or Persian lambs—are sold abroad and bring in about seventeen million dollars a year: shown above is one of the steps in the processing of the skins as it is done in northern Afghanistan.

22. *Old curio shop* in Afghanistan sells swords, lamps, bowls, and jewelry worn by women of nomad tribes. In such shops one finds a fascinating display of traditional Afghan crafts.

◀21. *Hammers on anvils* are a familiar sound throughout Afghanistan, where sickles, ploughs, and shoes for horses and donkeys are made by hand.

23. *Hookahs* made of bright blue pottery for passing tobacco smoke through water; they are also made of metal. The traditional "Persian blue" glaze is still used for this pottery fired in Istalif, not far from Kabul.

24. *Another curio shop* displays old-fashioned hand-guns of the arquebus type and a kind of lute; there are several such shops in Kabul catering chiefly to tourists.

25. *Nan-vendors* offer the country's staple food; usual working-class breakfast is a loaf of this bread and a cup of tea—freshly baked, *nan* is delicious but not very digestible.

26. *Melons* are plentiful—and fragrant—throughout the month of August; Marco Polo decided that the melons of northern Afghanistan were the world's finest.

27. *Kabul street-scene:* the day is Friday, the Muslim sabbath and day of rest, so people don their best clothes—and their prettiest *chadris*—to stroll through this bazaar in one of the suburbs of Kabul, a fascinating city which, ever since the invasion of Darius in 520 B.C., has been exposed to the influence of widely different ethnic groups.

28. *Masjid-i-Shah-do-Shamshira* (Mosque of the Two-sworded King), on the banks of the Kabul River, built at the beginning of this century, stands on the site of an older mosque, which in turn replaced a far older Hindu temple; the "King" is an Islamic commander who fought the Hindus with a sword in either hand.

29. *Column* (*see previous page*) commemorating those who fell in the 1924 rebellion; they gave their lives, says the inscription, in the struggle against ignorance. The fortress of the ancient city of Kabul stretches up the mountainside.

30. *Kabul River,* flowing through the heart of the city of Kabul, is the "mother" of city life. Here, at sunset, a lone man kneels on a bank of the Kabul River and raises his hands in fervent prayer.

31. *"Salaam 'Aleikum!"*—Peace be with you—is the standard greeting in all muslim countries: it is usually followed by prolonged formal requests about the health of all members of the two families.

32. *Busy new section* of Kabul, photographed at dusk: here are some of the city's best hotels and airline offices as well as government buildings.

33. *Waiter* from the Khyber Restaurant poses in front of a portrait of the King, His Majesty Muhammad Zahir Shah.

35. *Kabul University* has four new buildings that were opened in 1964 and about 3,300 students; there are four American teaching teams and a teacher-training project.

34. *Students* on their way to school. Unfortunately, Afghanistan still has far to go in educational facilities, and not many students get beyond junior high school; partly due to a shortage of teachers.

36. *Kabul River scene:* beneath a suspension bridge, children play while women do their laundry and wash their dishes; the river has always been the life-blood of the city.

37. *Buddha,* over twenty feet high,▶ carved in a cliff in the Valley of Kakrak, east of Bamiyan.

38. *Valley of Bamiyan (see overleaf)*, photo- ▶
graphed from the top of the 175-foot
Buddha: in the foreground is a bazaar, then
beyond the fields a quiet village surrounded
by trees; atop the hill on the right is a hotel,
while in the distance can be seen the Koh-i-
Baba mountains, snow-covered the year-
around. The river rises in the Hindu Kush.

39. *Tallest Buddha* in the world, the figure stands 175 feet; the rock is soft and porous, which facilitated the carving—and also the mutilation practiced by the Muslims.

40. *Drapery* was made of cords fastened to the statue with wooden pegs and covered with mud and straw, then coated with a kind of cement and painted.

41. *Ear of Buddha,* gives some idea of the colossal scale in which the figure was conceived. A decorated corridor winds around the head of the figure.

42—43. *Paintings* from the niche around the Buddha's head, which was once entirely covered with Buddhist devotional art; the few that remain, although badly damaged, are much admired and compare favorably with the Sassanid and Gupta paintings, and the famous cave-paintings of Ajanta.

44. *Pendentives* that permit one of the square rooms in the Bamiyan caves to be covered by a round dome are painted with countless figures of the Buddha.

45. *Seated Buddha,* with painted niche: the photograph was made with a telescopic lens, since there is no longer any way to climb this Buddha.

46. *Ceiling* in a Buddhist grotto: this type of ceiling is frequently encountered in Bamiyan and elsewhere in Afganistan and is still to be found in farmhouses in Nuristan, deep in the Hindu Kush; it may well have been an original architectural design of ancient Afghanistan.

47. *Bamiyan Bazaar* is all that remains of what must once have been one of the greatest bazaars of Asia: "There are more than ten monasteries and more than a thousand priests," wrote Hsüan-tsang in the year 632.

48. *Nomad family* passes listlessly through Bamiyan along a road that probably connected it with the oasis kingdoms of the north. People are still living in the ruins that the devastating Mongols left behind.

49. *Ruined Castle* of Qala-i-Dokhtar (Castle of the Daughter), betrayed to the Mongols, according to Bamiyan legend, by the vengeful daughter of its king; once having entered, they put the faithless girl to death.

50. *Five Dams of 'Ali:* Hazaras who live in the area believe that Caliph 'Ali, Mohammed's son-in-law, constructed five dams here for the relief of the farmers who were suffering from a shortage of water.

93

51. *Khwaja-Muhammad-Parsa Mosque,* standing in ruins at Balkh, the modern name for ancient Bactria, the capital of the Greco-Bactrian Empire, and then one of the world's greatest cities. Here Zoroaster was born and here Alexander the Great is said to have first met the beautiful Roxana.

52. *Bala Hissar,* the Bactrian citadel at
Balkh: little remains of what was once the
vast and imposing citadel of this world
capital, and no revealing archaeological
excavations have been made. Both Genghis
Khan and Tamerlane besieged the city.

53. *Castle walls* at Balkh of the Kushan Period (second to third century A.D.); the date is revealed by the arrowhead-shaped holes in the wall, which was later used by Muslims as a base for the construction of a higher wall. French archaeologists have been at work here.

54. *Balkh Teahouse,* proving that ancient Bactria, despite all its vicissitudes, is still a living city. Afghans love tea—it seems to flow constantly, along with the conversation. The teapots were made in Japan.

55. *Blue Mosque* at Mazar-i-Sharif that houses the tomb of Caliph 'Ali—or so the claim goes. There is another tomb of 'Ali at Najaf, in southern Iraq, and since he died nearby, Najaf's claim seems the more convincing. The mosque at Mazar is a lovely building, and the city itself has taken over Balkh's former pretensions to control in the district.

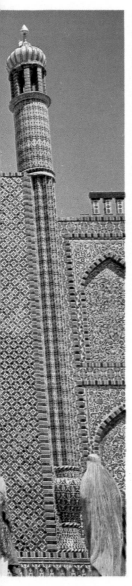

57. *Front wall* of the Mosque, showing the incredibly intricate and delicate patterns baked into the tiles. Although not themselves old, they are in the old tradition.

56. *Entrance* to the Mosque—men and women alike are extremely devout in Afghanistan; the colors of the tiles and the colors of the women's *chadris* seem to have sprung from the same source.

101

58. *Inner door* leading to the sacred precincts of the tomb itself; the women, having offered their prayers, are about to leave; the little boy on the right is putting on his shoes, which he had taken off when he entered the Mausoleum.

59. *Minaret* at Queen
Gawhar-Shad's *mad-
rassa* (or place of
learning), part of the
giant complex of
buildings erected in
Herat in the fifteenth
century at the com-
mand of Queen
Gawhar-Shad, or
Happy Pearl, wife of
Shah Rukh, Tamer-
lane's youngest son.
One of the most
remarkable women in
history, she reigned
for over fifty years,
maintained the bound-
aries of Tamerlane's
kingdom, and was one
of the most bountiful
patrons of the arts
the world has ever
known. Her minaret
is a fitting monument
to a great woman.

60. *Gazargah,* the most famous shrine in
Herat, contains the tomb of Khwaja Ansari,
the poet and philosopher who was born in
Herat in 1006 and died there in 1088. This
entrance to the shrine was reconstructed in
1428, at the order of Shah Rukh, by an
architect named Zainuddin, who so revered
Ansari that he asked to be buried facing the
shrine, with his tombstone in the form of a
kneeling dog. It may be seen in the left of
the plate above.

61. *Ramparts* of Herat dominate the bazaar: the city has been a bone of contention for over 2,500 years, from Cyrus, Darius, and Alexander to the British and the Persians in the last century. Afghan soldiers are still stationed on the ramparts.

62. *Covered reservoir,* sixty feet square, is a major monument of Herat, built in 1634 by Hasan Khan Shamlu, a governor ruling under the Safavid Dynasty. Light comes from a hole in the ceiling; the old man is pouring water into a goat-skin bag.

63. *Great Mosque* at Herat is the Masjid-i-Jami, or Friday Mosque, which was already famous in the tenth century. Several times destroyed and reconstructed, the present form of the Mosque is essentially that given it in the year 1200 by Sultan Ghiyasuddin-i-Ghori. The *madrassa,* or religious school, attached to the Mosque, the entrance to which is shown here, has about 50 students. The day of our group's visit, the marble in the inner courtyard was too hot to walk on in bare feet; the students, we noticed, as soon as a lesson ended, rushed out to buy ice cream from a vendor stationed right in front of the school.

65. *Tiles* are prepared for baking at a workroom within the Masjid Mosque; the methods used are those that have always been used.

66. *Persian blue* tiles have inlaid sentences taken from the Koran and famous Persian and Afghan poets. Strong Persian influence suggests Herat's strategic role as the gateway to Iran.

◄64. *Courtyard* of Masjid Mosque has a great well in one corner, equipped with a pump. Here two girls are filling utensils of very different vintage: modern polyethylene and traditional hammered metal.

111

67. *Shop* in a Herat bazaar: we were
surprised to see piles of boxes marked
"Made in Japan."

68. *Castle ruins* seen through an archway in Bust, the modern name for ancient Lashkargah, the winter capital of the Ghazni court. Seen from a great distance, across the desert of southern Afghanistan, the castle drifted before our eyes like a mirage.

69. *Near Kandahar,* the chief city of southern Afghanistan, stand a number of very ancient ruins, like the remains of the castle shown above.

70. *Desert flowers,* photographed on the dry, dusty, desolate road between Kandahar and Herat.

71. *Long ago* this must have been a room in the palace of Shahr-i-Kona (Old City); now it stands open to the desert sun and winds—being made of mud, it now returns to mud.

72. *Ahmad Shah,* the eighteenth-century empire-builder, laid out the square, walled city of Kandahar; his tomb (shown here) stands in the north-east corner of the eighteenth-century city.

73. *Tile-work* in the Ahmad Shah mausoleum might seem vulgar to some critics, but it unquestionably shows Afghan vitality and not Persian romanticism in execution.

74. *Chihil Zina*—the Forty Steps—cut by
the Mughal emperor Babur in the side of
a hill (upper left in photograph), on the
western outskirts of Kandahar. At the top
of the steps is a record of Babur's conquests
in India—and a breathtaking, panoramic
view of Kandahar and the countryside
around. As the Forty Steps is also a
military installation, we were not permitted
to take photographs from the summit.

75. *Old man* standing in front of a Ghazni tomb, southwest of Kabul. Because of the hardness and austerity of their lives, Afghans often look older than their years—but in their expressions the pride they feel in the fact that they are Afghans may always be read. The tomb in the background is one of the remains of the time when Ghazni, under Sultan Mahmud, was one of the great cities of the world, with splendid buildings and an imperial court that attracted scientists and poets, including Firdausi.

76. *Alauddin,* the World Burner, set fire to Ghazni; and the Moroccan traveler, Ibn Battuta, wrote after his visit, "Ghazni is now a desolate village surrounded by ruins." This stately minaret is one of them.

77. *Italian archaeologists* recently made investigations that indicate there is still a lot to be found in Ghazni—such as this mausoleum on a hilltop, with half a dozen marble tombs.

78. *Sultan Mahmud,* the hero of Ghazni, lies in this humble mausoleum; perhaps a more fitting tribute is the fact that the nearby dam and *karez* both bear his name.

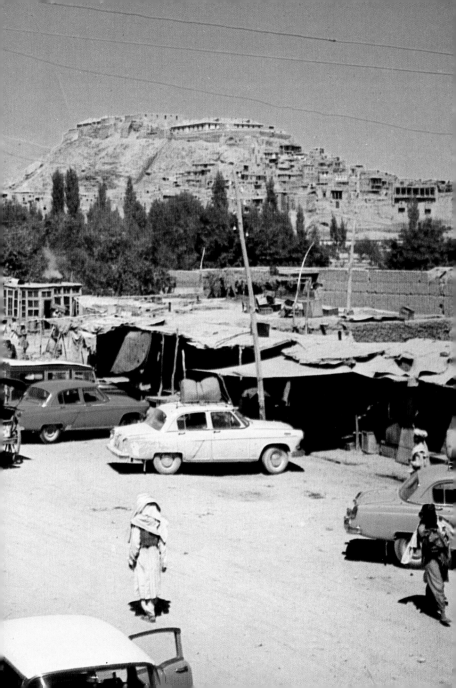

◄79. *Ghazni Bazaar* (*see previous page*), with the fortress in the background. It was an important fortified position a thousand years ago, and is still in use today: the army of Afghanistan maintains a military base there. Automobiles parked in front of the bazaar belong mainly to visitors from Kabul.

80. *Water!* How plentiful it is in some places, how scarce in others—and when it is scarce, how much it costs, in terms of human toil and trouble as well as money. Here water from a *karez* (an underground channel) is on its way to a village to sustain its life—and the life of the nomad tribes as well, who pitch their tents, the dark spots on the horizon, and water their flocks.

81. *Cleaning a karez* is hard work and must be done regularly to clear the entrance of earth. A cleaning team usually consists of four men who, because the work is also dangerous, must get along together. Watching the operation is the village *mullah,* a muslim spiritual leader.

82. *Village elders* opposed our desire to go down into a *karez* (because of the danger involved), but we finally secured their approval. With helmets, headlamps, spurs, hooks, and rope, we descended—without mishap—to a depth of almost fifty feet.

83. *Camels* belonging to a nomad tribe filling up at a *karez*.

127

84. *Karez water* flowing toward a village is strictly rationed, and its course is changed frequently. The unglazed earthen pot the girl is carrying will sweat—and so keeps the water cool.

85. *Deserts of Afghanistan* would be wholly
desert but for the *karez* system of irrigation,
and the entire village lives by it and depends
on it. Here children have come to play
beside the water. The boys posed willingly,
but the little girl only shyly faced the camera.

87. *Cut wheat* is piled high on the ground in the shape of a doughnut; then it is threshed by plodding oxen. Shown in the plate is the result of a year's hard work by the farmers.

◀86. *Mister Bones* was our nickname for this kind and affable gentleman who was such a good friend to us and so helpful. We lived in one corner of the land-owner's extensive house, seen in the background. Mr. Bones has just unloaded wheat from the donkey to be carried to the threshing floor.

88. *Winnowing* is accomplished by the ancient method of throwing the wheat high in the air with a many-pronged instrument. The chaff is blown away by the wind; the grains drop straight to the ground.

89. *Roadside teahouse:* teahouses, ▶ found everywhere throughout Afghanistan, are restaurants during the day and hostels at night. The proprietor of this one keeps a dog, which is unusual in Afghanistan as in most muslim countries. Nomads are the exception: they all have fierce watchdogs.

90. *Butcher-shop,* in a corner of a bazaar: after his stock has been sold out, the butcher gets another sheep, which he kills ritually, and then puts it up for sale—almost all of it, including the head and hoofs.

91. *Prayers* are offered by the roadside: Muslims are told to pray five times a day, no matter where they are or what they may be doing. Here a bus has stopped to let its passengers fulfill their obligations.

92. *Hookahs* are always provided in every teahouse, and patrons—like this boy—may make use of them whenever they like. The tobacco is strong even after it passes through water; generally only two or three puffs are taken.

93. *Old woman* basking in the sun in front of the thick mud wall of her house, where she was born and lived all her life; the spectacles she wears are a rare sight in an Afghan village.

94. *Bride and groom:* 'Ali, aged twenty-six, a tenant-farmer, with his bride of seventeen. He had to pay money and sheep to her family; lacking these, a man may remain a bachelor. Rich men may take several wives.

95. *Young lad* of thirteen was ▶ of tremendous help to us in our village study. Highly intelligent, he is still attending school and speaks both Pashto and Persian. He is shown here with his little sister.

96—97. *Building a house* is not a very difficult or protracted affair in an Afghan village: mud bricks are dried in the sun, built into walls, then covered with mud plaster. A man can produce about 200 bricks a day, and it takes only about 1,500 to complete a house. Lumber is scarce and costly.

98. *Village house,* behind its impene-
trable mud wall, is likely to shelter
numerous members of a large family:
brothers and cousins, with their wives
and progeny as well as their livestock.
There is also a granary, of course.

99—100. *Red hammock* holds a few-months' old baby being tended by brothers and sisters. Babies generally go uncovered below the waist.

101. *Children* play together ▶ until they are around six; then girls are confined to the house. After the age of fifteen, no one—boy or girl—may enter the inner court of a house that is not his own, even though it may be that of a close relative.

102. *Dough* for bread is kneaded by the wife of Abdul Qadir, an Army officer. Only man in the village with four wives, he has taken one to his Army post; the others live harmoniously together with their seventeen children.

103. *National independence* is celebrated during the last week in August, when the whole of the country takes on a festive mood. The National Stadium in Kabul is the scene of mass games, various types of sports contests, and native dances. The government uses the festival to foster a spirit of nationalism.

104. *Girls* marching across stadium during Independence Week come mainly from upper-class families; they will receive all the education Afghanistan has to offer and will be expected to help in the modernization of the country.

105. *Veils* have been discarded by many women and girls of Afghanistan, but sexes nevertheless do not mingle in the stands. A woman member of our group is in the center, wearing a straw hat.

106. *Tribal dances,* being per-
formed during Independence cere-
monies in the Stadium, require
elaborate and colorful costumes,
intricately embroidered.

107. *Malik* (*see overleaf*) is a village ▶
head who once administered his
entire village as though it was an
independent country; now he is
an elected government official who
mediates disputes and looks after
Army conscription.

THIS BEAUTIFUL WORLD